The Real Gard
Sch

Learn how to troubleshoot
every year

Dubravko Zivkovic

A Christmas tree that has outlived its usefulness lies naked on the compost heap as another year begins in this extraordinary cycle of birth, death, and rebirth in January. While you load a seven-foot Douglas fir and a dried poinsettia into your wheeled bin on a crisp January morning, take a moment to reflect on new beginnings.

Hans Christian Andersen was the one who said that just living isn't enough and that to thrive, you need sunshine, freedom, and a little flower. However, keep in mind that there are no flowers without tools, and there are no tools without a place to store them. Which brings us to this year's first job.

Recover your tools from beneath the clutter that has gathered in your garage over the winter. Utilize a number 2 oily John Innes rag to clean them.

You will find a forgotten box of moldy dahlias, glads, and other bulbs that you diligently wintered in your damp garage while searching. Put them away. Make arrangements to have your lawnmower's cutting blades sharpened. When you discover that it has been stolen, as have the majority of your tools, go buy a new one. Install a new lock on your garage.

9 The days are short, and it can get very cold at night. Even the most timid birds and mammals are active because they need to find food, and if the weather is really bad, even normally nocturnal animals may venture

outside during the day. Because of this, now is a great time to down the bottle of Stag's Breath from New Year's Eve and spend the gloomy afternoons in your greenhouse shooting pot shots at hedgehogs and badgers.

Planning big goals and fantasizing about winning gold medals at the Chelsea Flower Show are best done in January. You should ask your son, who is eight years old, to show you the Garden Planner CD-ROM that he got you for Christmas. Now is the time to plant jasmine, heather, and other winter-flowering shrubs.

Pansies, geraniums, and other early flowers can be seeded. If the CD-ROM "fails to install on Windows 3.1," you can get a refund.

Twist up with a goodly heap of customary

furthermore, dependable plant and seed lists.

Purchase new devices, lawnmower and

interactive media PC.

On the off chance that you are a novice who feels

overpowered by the decision of

cultivating hardware, here are the

essentials you should get everything rolling:

One short, pointed object for removing weeds.

One long sharp thing for jabbing out

weeds when your back is sore.

A single small container for weeds.

One enormous holder (for example a wheely receptacle)

for exhausting the little holder when

it is brimming with weeds.

a can of gasoline to light a fire when your wheelbarrow is full.

Whether it's a weeding cushion, gloves, or hoe, every gardener has a favorite tool. In any case, picking the

right planting clothing is significantly more

significant. Have you seen how

manufacturers generally wear creator shirts?

Wear the most expensive clothing you can afford if you want to avoid getting muddy. The statement you want to make is: expensive-durable'. On the off chance that your

neighbor sees you getting down and

grimy in a £125 Burberry polo shirt, he'll

assume that you own twenty more.

The garden appears somewhat barren in January, but there are a few spots where the beauty of nature is always present that you might enjoy visiting. Use your brand-new personal computer while you remain inside.

This winter, why not brush up on your Latin skills? The Latin system of naming flowers and plants is not nearly as complicated as it may at first appear. Color, habitat, season, scent, growth, and aesthetic are all conveyed by the words. You can build an impressive vocabulary at your digitalis endia by learning twenty Latin words.

15 A green flower from the southern hemisphere, for instance, might be called viridis australis. Viridis patens is the name for a green plant that spreads (which, let's face it, you can use to describe most plants); red and

fragrant' is rubens fragrens; whereas the term "wild and grows in pastures" is feris pastoralis. Sementem needs very little upkeep; acid lounge does well indoors when the soil has a pH of less than 7; furthermore, a

express that will show up as often as possible in

this book, naboreus gardenia, scarcely

needs any interpretation.

16 JANUARY: THE ACCIDENTAL GARDENER If you don't want to learn all those Latin names, memorize some of the track listings on an album by Jimi Hendrix. On Voodoo Child,

there are several plausible examples: Spanish Castle Magic, Little Wing, Purple Haze, Foxy Lady, Wild Thing, Izabella, and Dolly Dagger.

Someone must have had rabies if they said that watering plants in the midday sun can burn them.

Water can't consume anything. In point of fact, it is widely acknowledged to be an efficient means of putting out fires.

Always keep in mind that your garden is just like everyone else's.

FEBRUARY

The crocus is quick to sprout

While winter's frosty ices hold influence

Tricking you that spring comes soon

Despite the fact that it's ages away

There's an old Russian precept that

says that more fills in the nursery than

the landscaper plants - alluding, obviously,

to each landscaper's most horrendously terrible adversary:

weeds. At the point when the year's most memorable weeds and

bothers begin to show up, it's essential to

get in a precautionary strike to forestall

them from overpowering you later. You'll end up knee-deep in sticky mud if you try to hoe out weeds. Renting a hydraulic PTO with a 500-gallon heavy-duty stainless steel spray tank, 35 GPM positive displacement pump, 0–800 PSI pressure gauge, and powerful mechanical agitation is the smartest option. Put some Wagner on the hi-fi, open the lounge window, and enter the battle!

There are just as many strategies for smuggling spent plutonium out of the former Soviet Union as there are for preventing pests from infesting your garden. A barrel of toxic mulch for your roses will be sold to you at your local petrochemical by-product outlet at no extra cost. Spread

thickly to guarantee inclusion. Studies indicate that selective weedkillers do not eradicate all weeds.

Keep in mind the gardener's lore that it's better to kill any wildlife than to save the plant it might be clinging to. In the event that you begin viewing as dead

squirrels, moles and deer in your

garden, or hear neighborhood news reports that

the water table has been debased,

then you'll realize you've done a

exhaustive work.

Nursery workers generally attempt to outshine each

other with their capacity to name until recently

unbelievable dangers, the ramifications

being that they've proactively taken quick

activity to kill bugs that you didn't

indeed, even know existed, while your nursery

is without a doubt pervaded. What fledgling

nursery workers don't understand is that the majority of

these names are made up by adding the

word 'fly', 'vermin', 'spot' or 'weevil' to

the finish of any word, generally a variety.

Consequently sawfly, whitefly, greenfly,

blackspot, lawnmite, shedfly, fencemite,

arseweevil, and so on.

February 22: THE ACCIDENTAL GARDENER The majority of seed packets contain over a hundred seeds. Be that as it may, do you truly mean

to establish 125 sunflowers this spring?

Instead, set aside about thirty dollars, and the next time someone asks you for money on the street, say, I won't give you money because I know you'll use it on junk food and alcohol, but kindly accept this seed with my love.

For maximum bloom production, winter-flowering pansies require a bright, sunny location. However paradise

knows how this should occur

while the weather conditions is still so

unusual. Begin tidying your

houseplants again once they start to

give indications of new development and keep

advising yourself that your Occasional

Full of feeling Problem will before long move along.

Ensure you safeguard the youthful shoots

arising out of your grass in regions

where you have established daffodils.

Until November, the house should be locked up for children and dogs.

Get ready vegetable plots. Plant your potato crops in garden compost that has been well-composed. Then ask yourself

why you just endured seven hours digging

to sustain such a modest and exhausting

vegetable. Plant asparagus beds next year, or construct a fiberglass pagoda.

Nail any branches that have been damaged by winter storms onto your trees and shrubs. Remove any branches from your neighbor's trees that are overhanging

your property and either toss them

over the wall or dump them in his skip.

A small garden can be made to appear larger in a variety of ways. The

best of these is pruning. Right now, trim fruit trees and other evergreens. Hard pruning is good for most plants. Salix x rubens "Basfordiana" is a radiant presence in any winter border due to their naked beauty. Now is the time to enjoy them, but prune the suckers back to their stubby little bases to teach them humility. Pruning should be done as close to the ground as your tools will allow, as a general rule. If you got a chainsaw for Christmas, use it to hard prune now so you can lay decking and a big plastic garden chess set down.

Pesticides don't harm the

climate. Simply put, they are chemicals positioned incorrectly.

Dig and burn when you're not sure.

We trundle around in wellington boots, lifting and dividing large clumps of herbaceous plants because spring is coming and flash frosts are killing the early shoots. After removing enough old woody stalks to fill your neighbor's skip, replant the three tiny specimens. To close the gap, get a cute Gandalf gargoyle or a small Japanese ornamental bridge.

Prepare to mow frequently. Your lawn will begin to grow quickly now, filling you with pride for several days in the middle of April before ants, pets, and children make it look like a soccer field from the Northern Counties League.

Did you know that ducks are slugs' natural prey? As the well-known adage goes, assuming you have such a large number of slugs the

odds are you have a lack of

ducks. So purchase a couple this month and

you'll before long can't escape duck keeping.

When gardening, you should always wear boots or sturdy shoes. You never know when your neighbor will show up and tell you to stop putting your garden waste in his skip. And it's always a blessing to be in your favorite pair of 10-eyelet leather boots with steel toecaps and three-row stitches when punches start flying. Additionally, when he unleashes his Staffordshire bull terrier, they provide the much-needed protection.

Your mother will visit for a week this month. The combination of dry heat and excessive watering from a bored and interfering relative will kill most of your houseplants because she will insist on having the heating on full power. While she slaves over Trevor Eve pouting his way through yet another cop drama on BBC1, you can expect to miss the first episode of the new series of Real Gardens on Channel 4.

On your way back from the garden center, pick a bright, crisp March morning to visit your attorney. It's time to rekindle the boundary dispute that appeared to have subsided over the winter now that spring has finally arrived. Additionally, in order to prevent the ducks from entering your naboreus gardenia, keep an eye out for holes in the hedge.

Your extravagant mail-request pelargoniums

ought to have shown up at this point. Put them in the conservatory in a pot and water them. If you don't have a conservatory, try spending less time in the garden and focusing on how to impress your boss instead. It's already way too late if you're retired.

Net out the duckweed from the lake

(this should be done much of the time, or it will

totally cover the outer layer of the

water and block out daylight). Now that I think about it, why bother when a heron took your ghost koi and shubunkin in October, leaving you with three huge golden orfe? And where is the sun anyway?

Frogs, newts and kids will likewise

show up in the lake this month. Children can't resist trying to drown themselves, no matter how many times you tell them not to go near water.

If not for the ducks, you could fill

in the lake with enormous stones until the

youngsters are more seasoned. You might pick an

shrewd split the difference and fill your

youngsters' pockets with so many

stones that they can't get off the couch.

In addition, oxygenating the water in your pond does not necessitate the purchase of a fountain. Simply bring the cat inside each morning. Before removing him once more, allow him to thrash around helplessly for five minutes. He will

benefit from the enthusiastic activity and

will circulate air through the lake simultaneously.